City Maps

The Reader's Digest Association, Inc.
Pleasantville, New York • Montreal

Project Editor: Carroll C. Calkins
Project Art Director: Richard Berenson
Produced in association with the H.M. Goushā Company

Copyright © 1981 The Reader's Digest Association, Inc.
Copyright © 1981 The Reader's Digest Association (Canada) Ltd.
Copyright © 1981 Reader's Digest Association Far East Ltd.
Philippine Copyright 1981 Reader's Digest Association Far East Ltd.
Maps Copyright © The H.M. Goushā Company

All rights reserved. Unauthorized reproduction,
in any manner, is prohibited.

Library of Congress Catalog Card Number 80-53041

ISBN 0-89577-095-4

Printed in the United States of America
Fifth Printing, May 1985

Contents

ALABAMA
Birmingham 3
Mobile 3
Montgomery ... 4

ARIZONA
Phoenix 4
Tucson 5

ARKANSAS
Little Rock 5

CALIFORNIA
Los Angeles 6
Sacramento 6
San Diego 7
San Francisco ... 8
San Jose 8

COLORADO
Colorado Springs 9
Denver 9

CONNECTICUT
Bridgeport 10
Hartford 10
New Haven ... 11

DELAWARE
Wilmington ... 11

DIST. OF COLUMBIA
Washington ... 12

FLORIDA
Fort Lauderdale 12
Jacksonville ... 13
Miami 13
Orlando 14
Palm Beach ... 16
Pensacola 15
St. Petersburg .. 14
Tampa 15
W. Palm Beach . 16

GEORGIA
Atlanta 16
Columbus 17

IDAHO
Boise 17

ILLINOIS
Chicago 19
Decatur 18
Moline 20
Peoria 18
Rockford 19
Rock Island ... 20

INDIANA
Evansville 20
Fort Wayne ... 21
Indianapolis ... 21

IOWA
Bettendorf 20
Davenport 20
Des Moines ... 22

KANSAS
Topeka 22
Wichita 23

KENTUCKY
Louisville 23
Lexington 24

LOUISIANA
Baton Rouge .. 24
New Orleans .. 25

MAINE
Portland 25

MARYLAND
Annapolis 26
Baltimore 26

MASSACHUSETTS
Boston 27
Springfield 27
Worcester 28

MICHIGAN
Detroit 28
Flint 29
Grand Rapids .. 29

MINNESOTA
Minneapolis ... 29
St. Paul 29

MISSISSIPPI
Jackson 30

MISSOURI
Columbia 30
Kansas City ... 31
St. Joseph 31
St. Louis 32

MONTANA
Great Falls 32
Helena 33

NEBRASKA
Fremont 33
Lincoln 34
Omaha 34

NEVADA
Las Vegas 35
Reno 35

NEW HAMPSHIRE
Concord 36
Manchester 36

NEW JERSEY
Atlantic City ... 37
Trenton 37

NEW MEXICO
Albuquerque .. 38
Santa Fe 38

NEW YORK
Albany 39
Buffalo 39
New York 40
Rochester 40
Syracuse 41
Utica 42

NORTH CAROLINA
Charlotte 42
Greensboro 43
Winston-Salem . 43

NORTH DAKOTA
Grand Forks ... 43

OHIO
Akron 44
Cincinnati 45
Cleveland 44
Toledo 46

OKLAHOMA
Lawton 46
Oklahoma City . 47
Tulsa 47

OREGON
Portland 48
Salem 48

PENNSYLVANIA
Erie 49
Harrisburg 49
Philadelphia ... 50
Pittsburgh 50
Scranton 51

RHODE ISLAND
Providence 51

SOUTH CAROLINA
Charleston 52
Columbia 52

SOUTH DAKOTA
Rapid City 53

TENNESSEE
Chattanooga ... 53
Knoxville 54
Memphis 54
Nashville 55

TEXAS
Amarillo 55
Austin 56
Dallas 57
Fort Worth 56
Houston 57
San Antonio ... 58
Wichita Falls .. 58

UTAH
Salt Lake City . 59

VERMONT
Burlington 59

VIRGINIA
Norfolk 60

WASHINGTON
Olympia 60
Seattle 61
Spokane 62
Tacoma 61

WEST VIRGINIA
Charleston 62

WISCONSIN
Madison 63
Milwaukee 63

WYOMING
Cheyenne 64
Laramie 64

Alabama

Birmingham

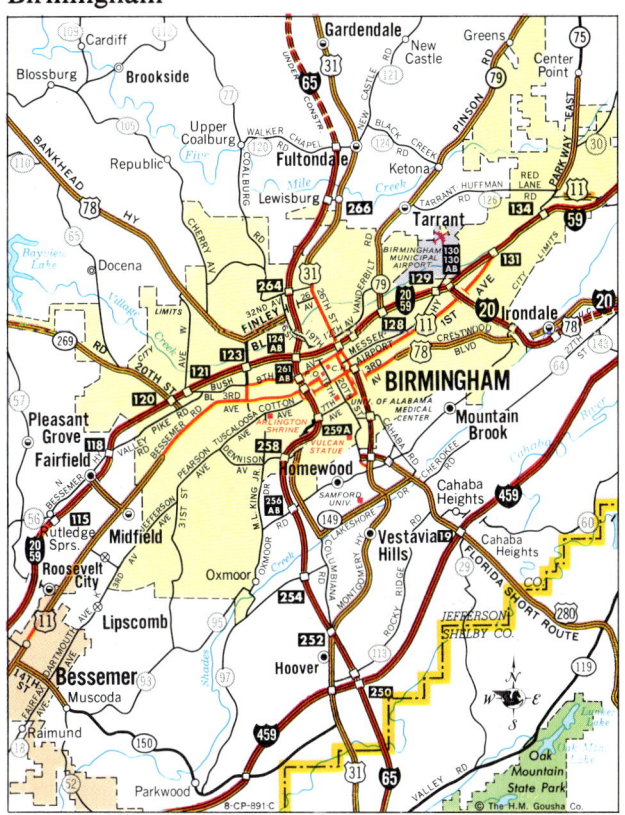

Mobile

Alabama
(continued)

Montgomery

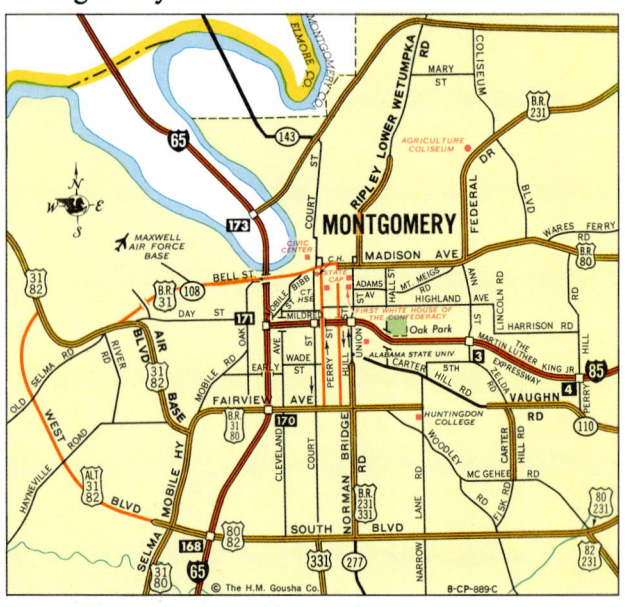

Arizona

Phoenix

Tucson

Arkansas

Little Rock

California

Sacramento

Los Angeles

San Diego

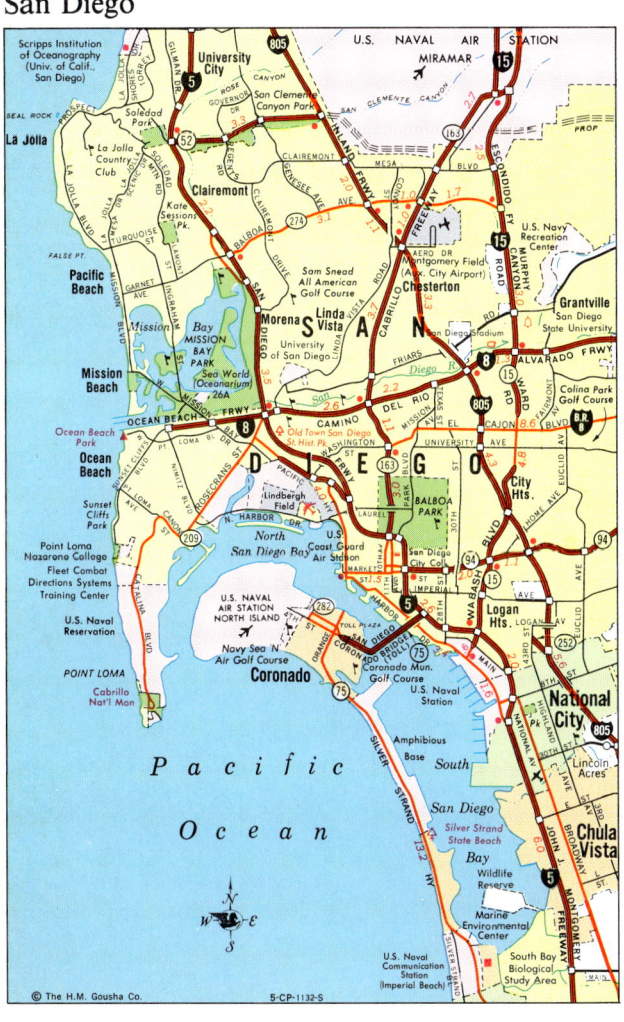

California
(continued)

San Francisco

San Jose

Colorado

Colorado Springs

Denver

Connecticut

Bridgeport

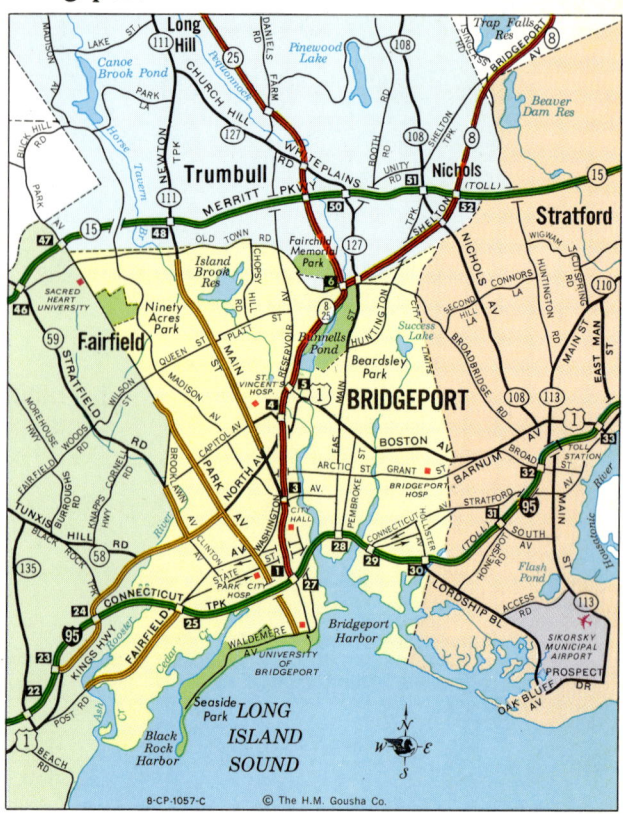

Hartford

New Haven

Delaware

Wilmington

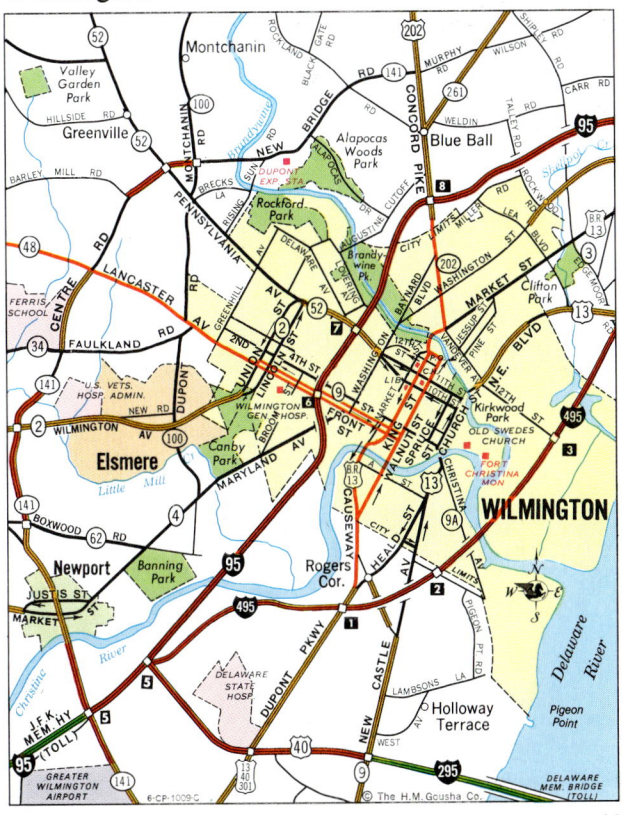

District of Columbia

Washington

Florida

Fort Lauderdale

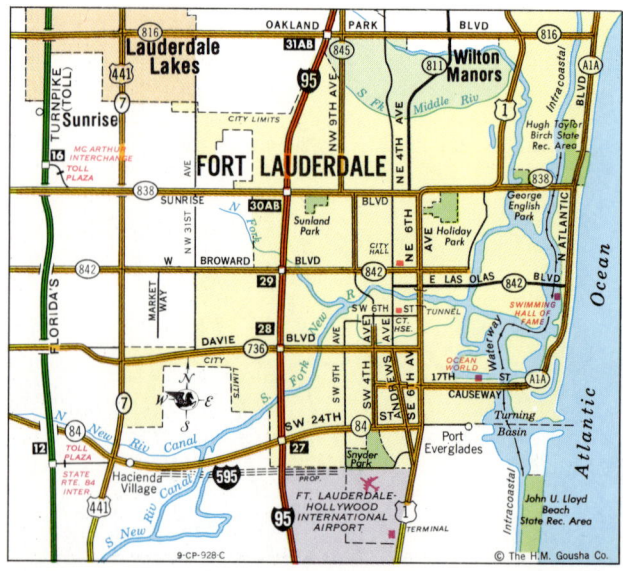

Jacksonville

Miami

Florida
(continued)

Orlando

Tampa, St. Petersburg

Pensacola

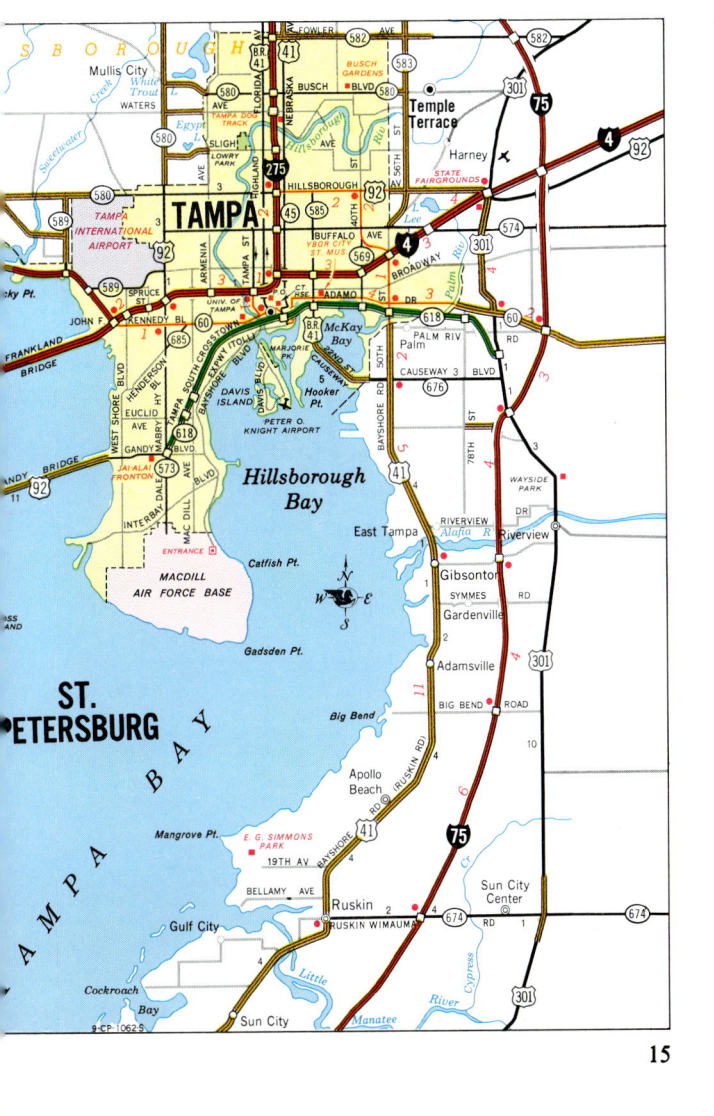

Florida
(continued)

West Palm Beach, Palm Beach

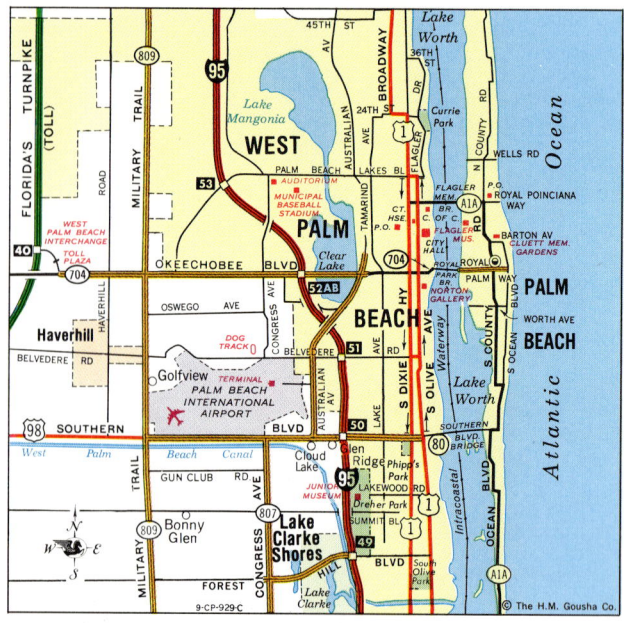

Georgia

Atlanta

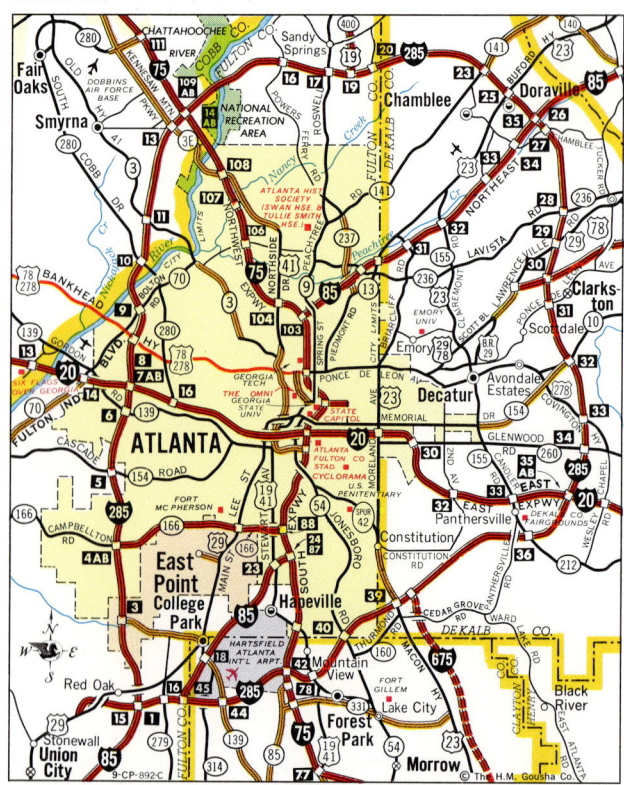

Columbus

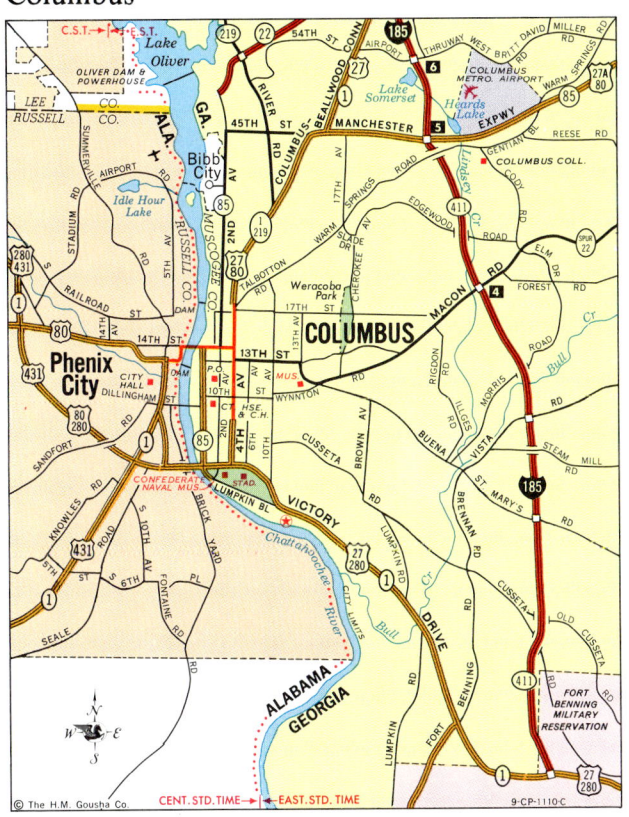

Idaho

Boise

Illinois

Decatur

Peoria

Chicago

Rockford

Illinois-Iowa

Quad Cities

Indiana

Evansville

Fort Wayne

Indianapolis

Iowa

Des Moines

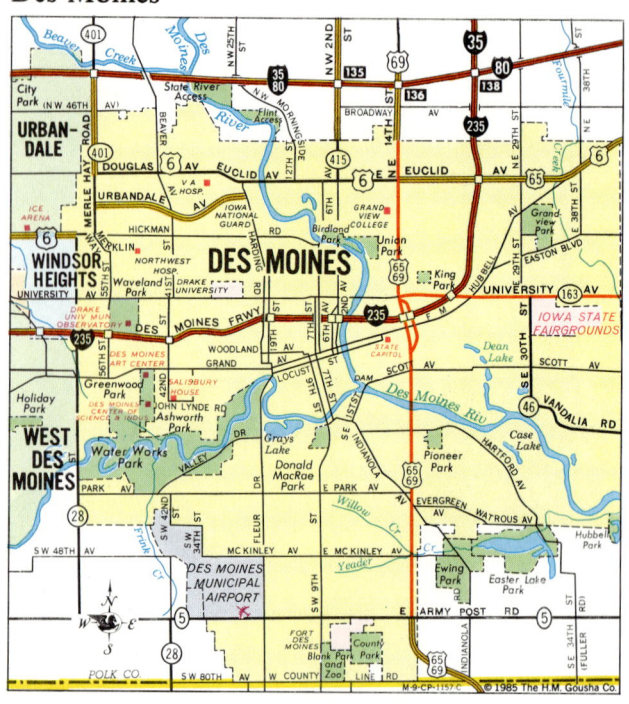

Kansas

Topeka

Wichita

Kentucky

Louisville

Kentucky
(continued)

Lexington

Louisiana

Baton Rouge

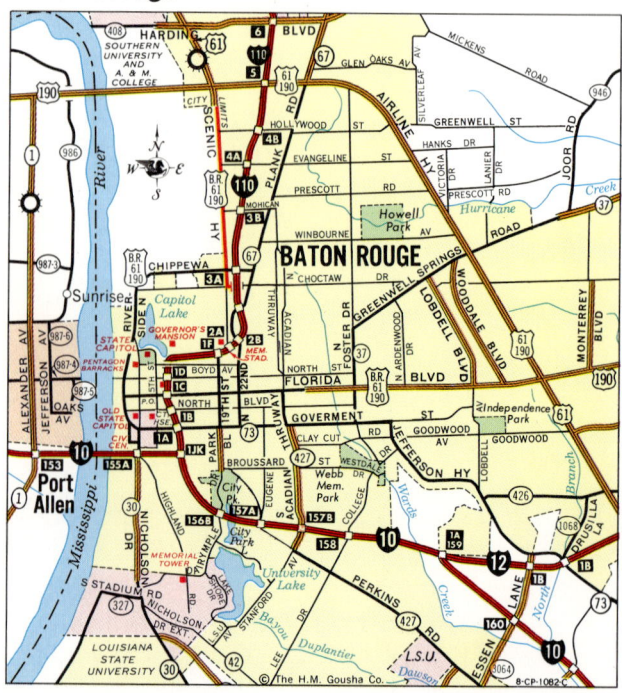

New Orleans

Maine

Portland

Maryland

Annapolis

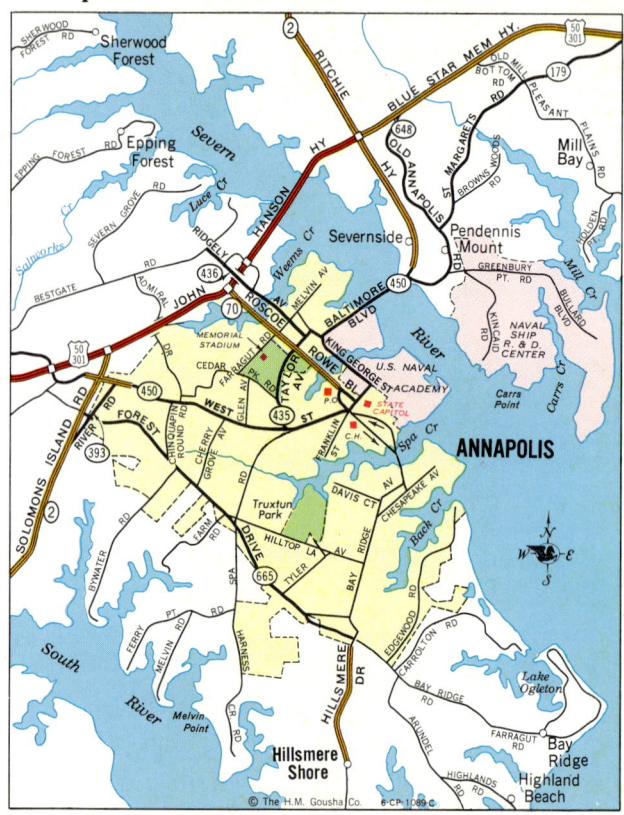

Baltimore

Massachusetts

Boston

Springfield

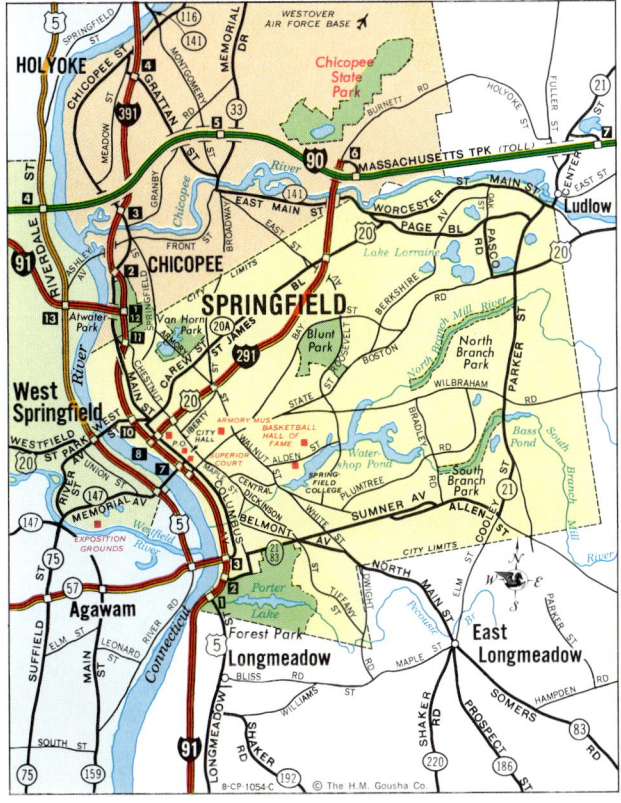

Massachusetts
(continued)

Worcester

Michigan

Detroit

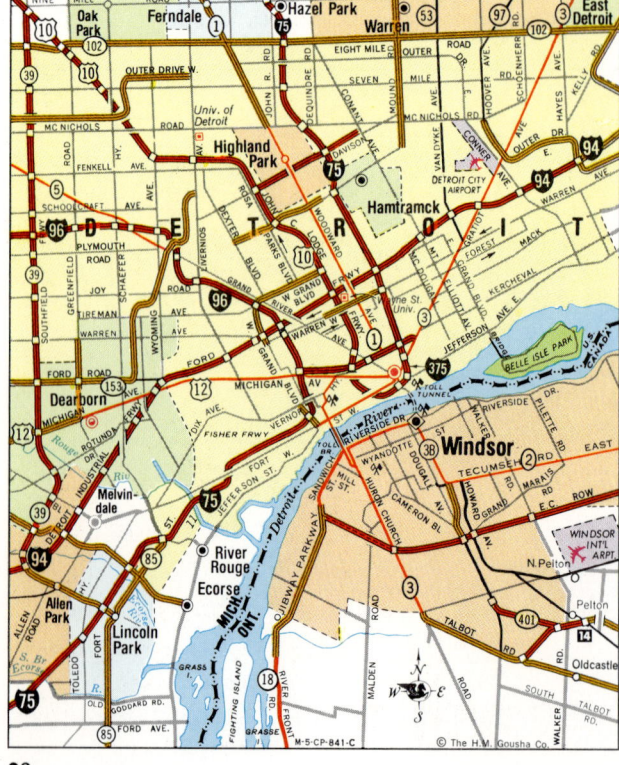

Flint

Grand Rapids

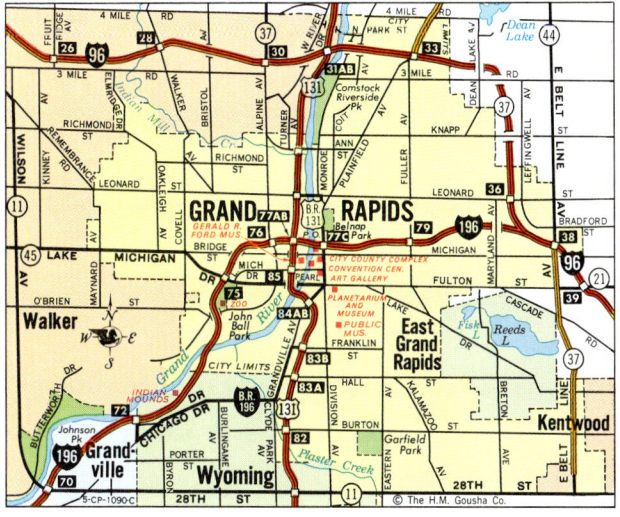

Minnesota

Minneapolis, St. Paul

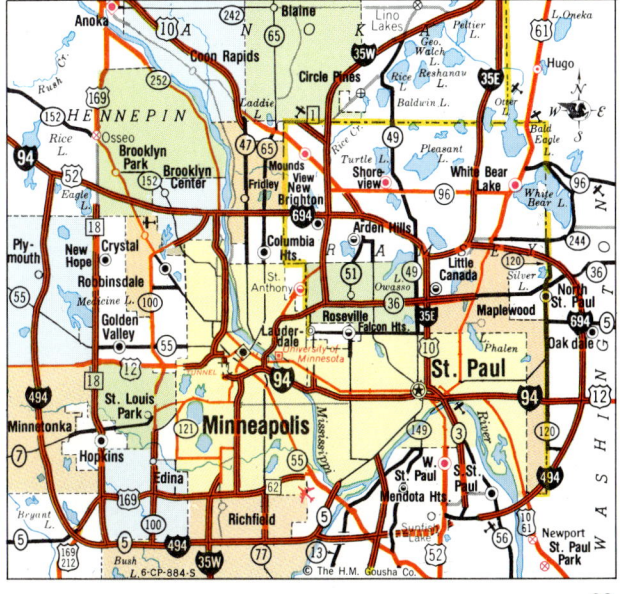

Mississippi

Jackson

Missouri

Columbia

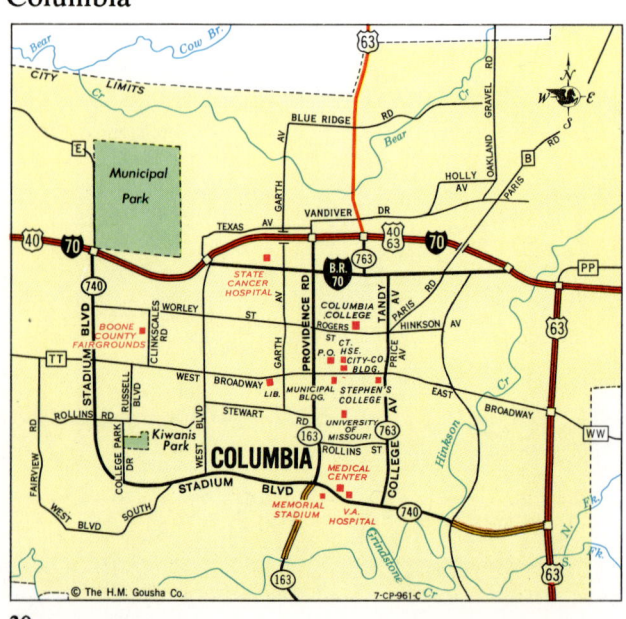

Kansas City

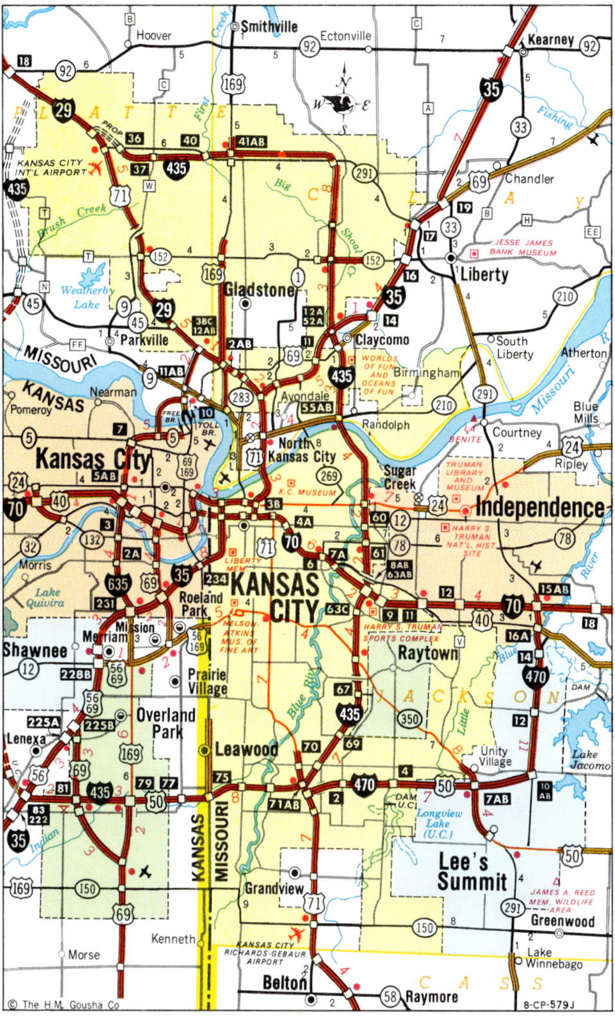

St. Joseph

Missouri
(continued)

St. Louis

Montana

Great Falls

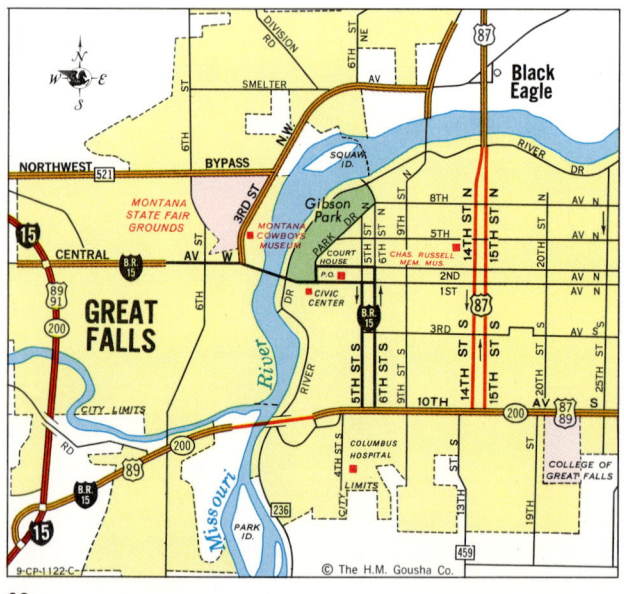

Helena

Nebraska

Fremont

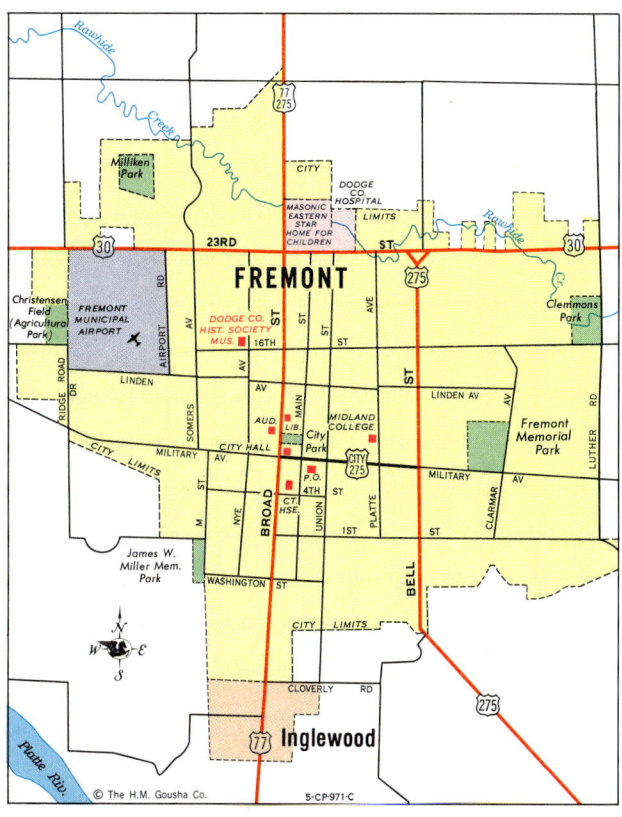

Nebraska
(continued)

Lincoln

Omaha

Nevada

Las Vegas

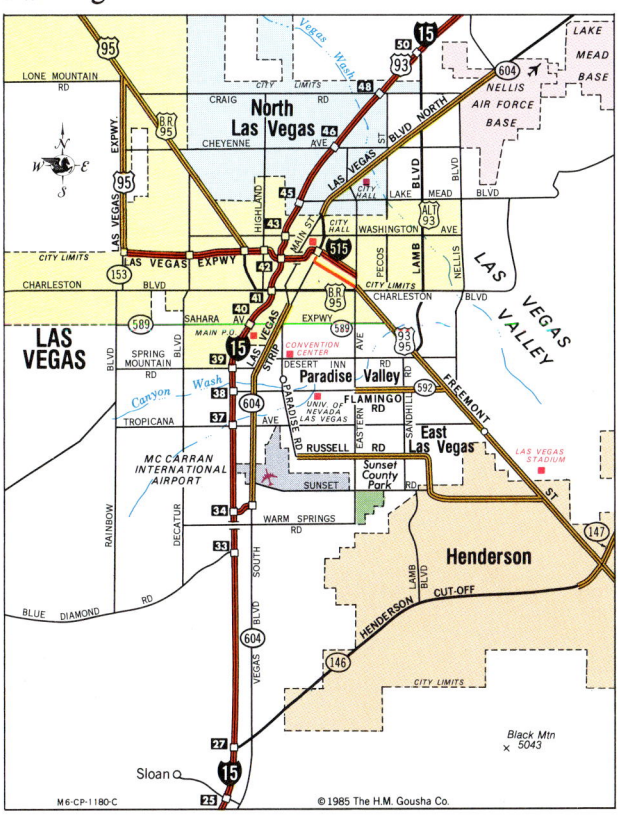

Reno

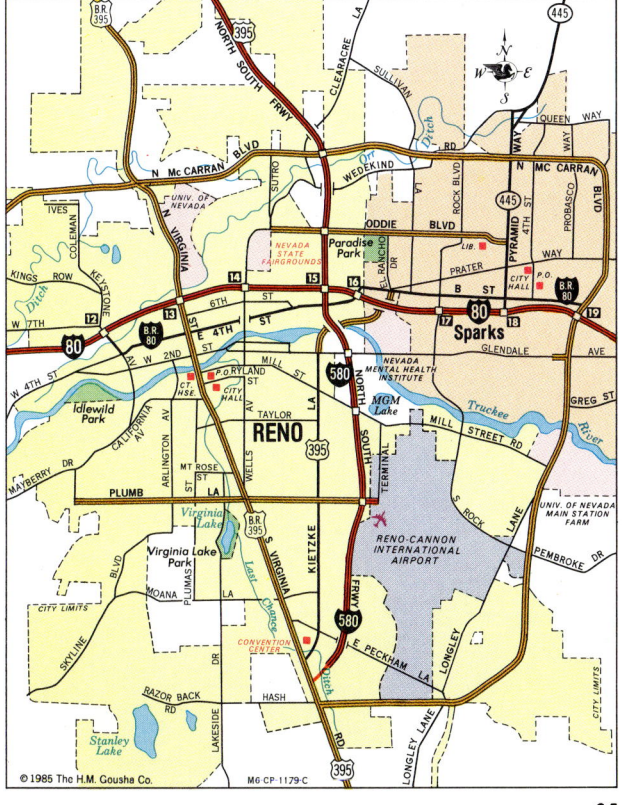

New Hampshire

Concord

Manchester

New Jersey

Atlantic City

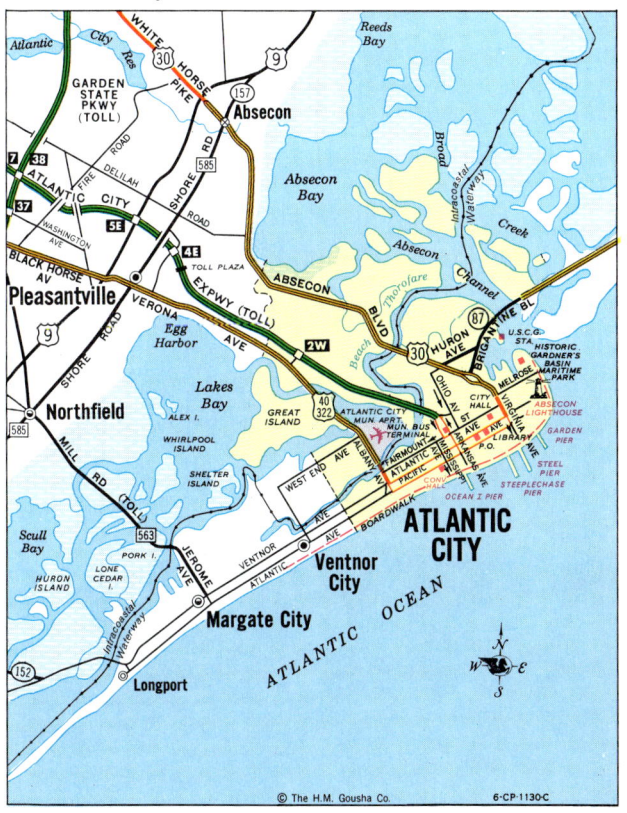

Trenton

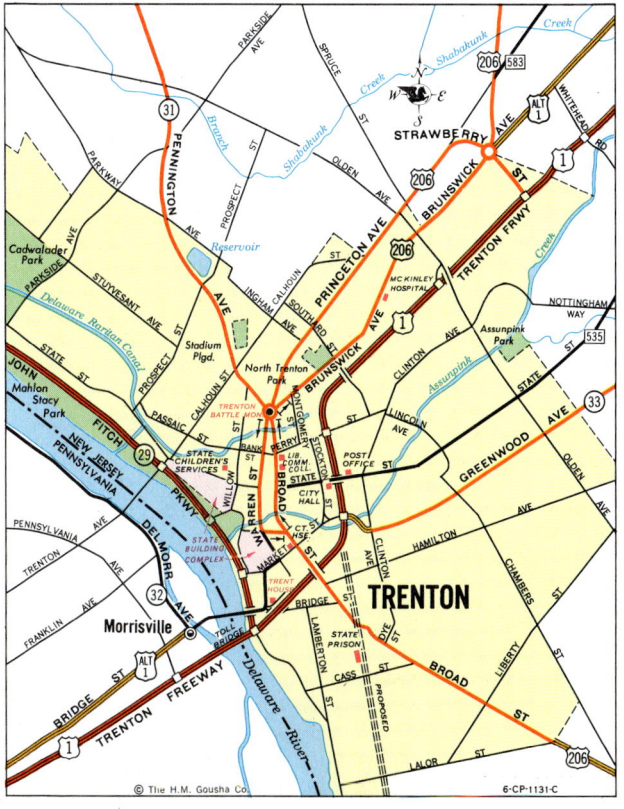

New Mexico

Albuquerque

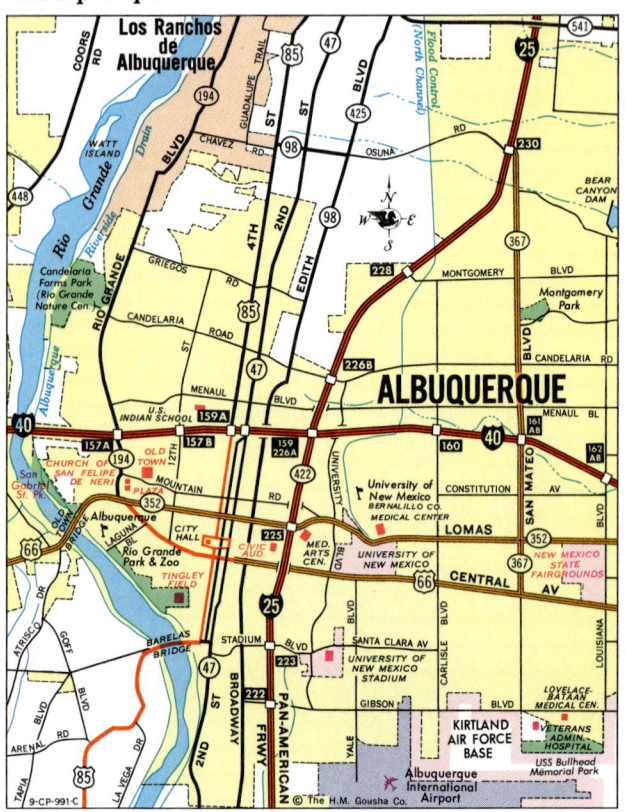

Santa Fe

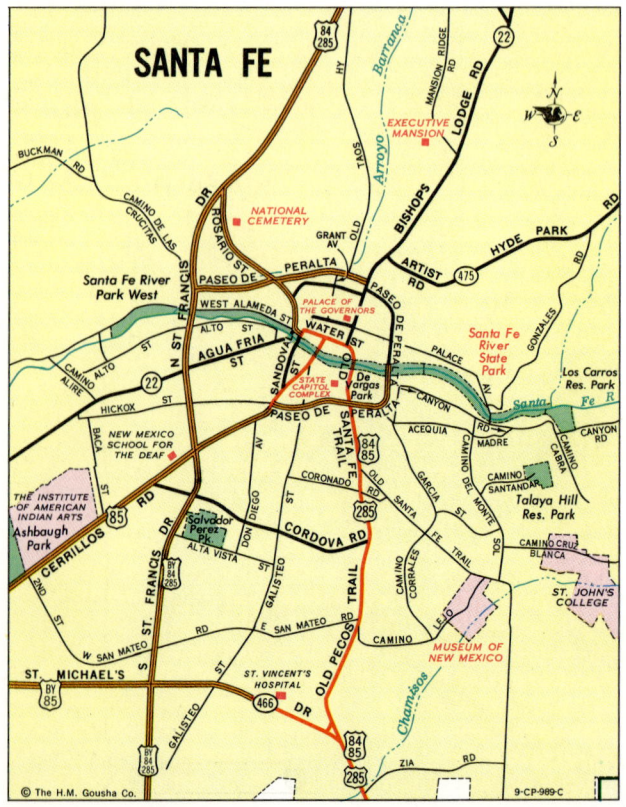

New York

Albany

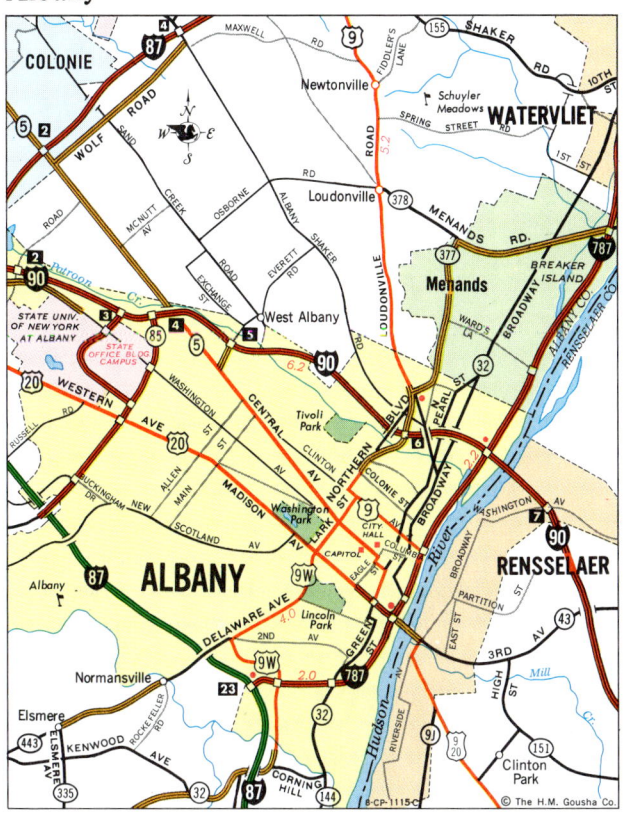

Buffalo

New York
(continued)

Rochester

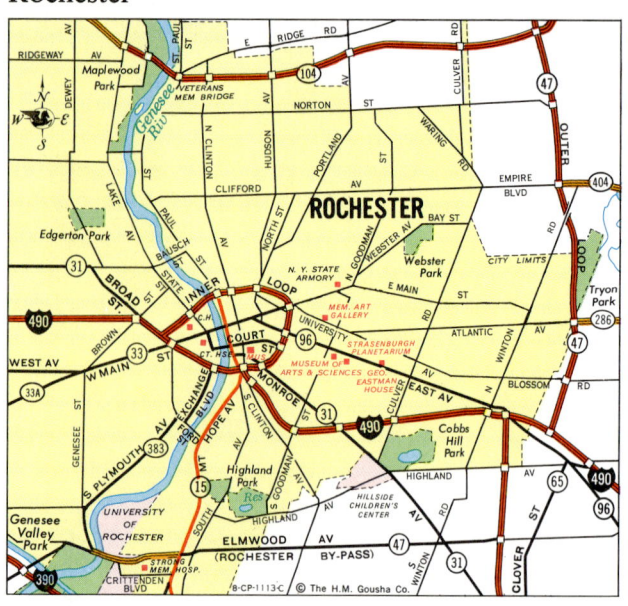

New York

Syracuse

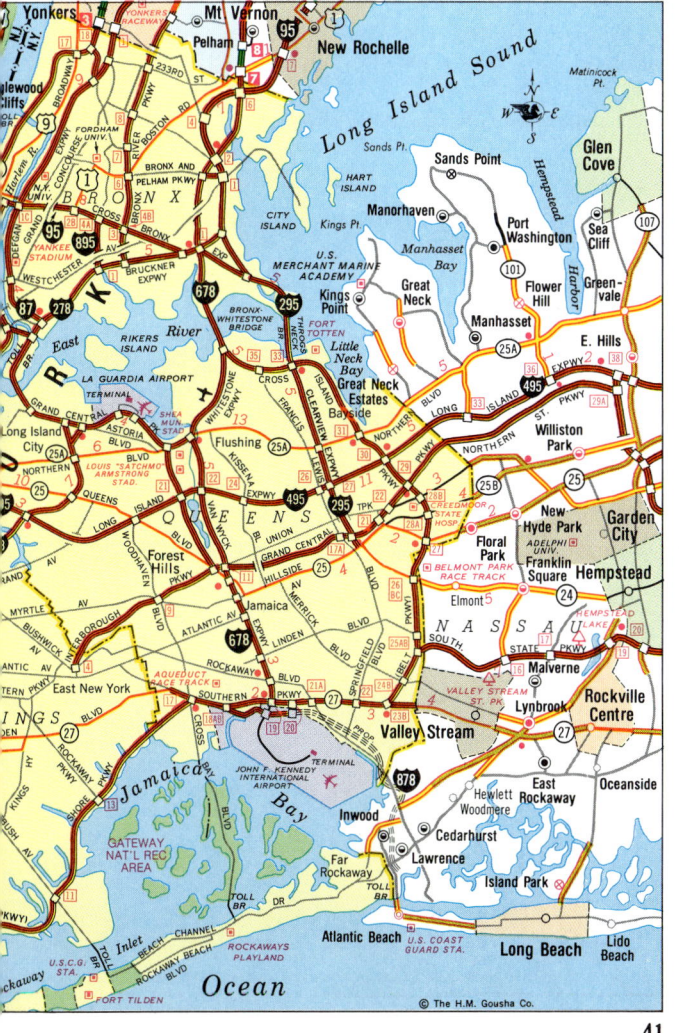

New York
(continued)

Utica

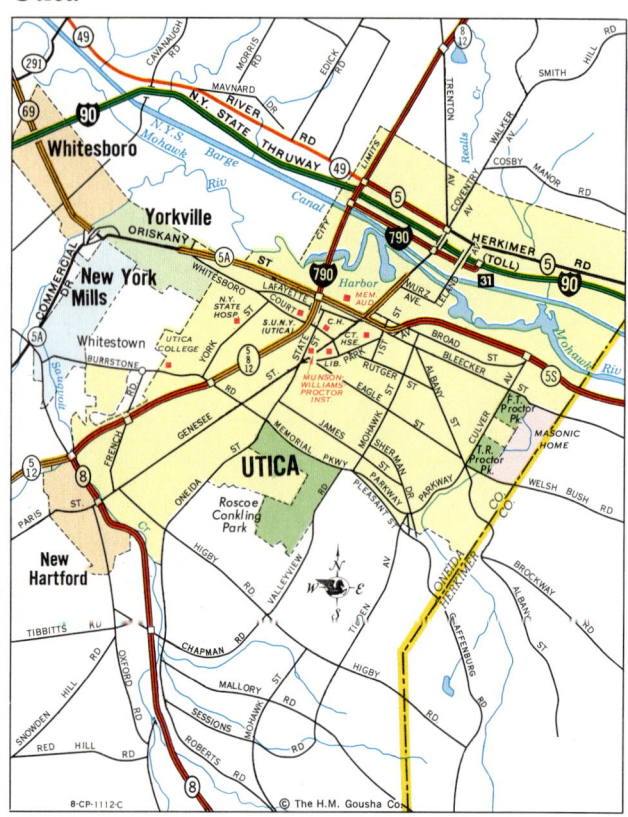

North Carolina

Charlotte

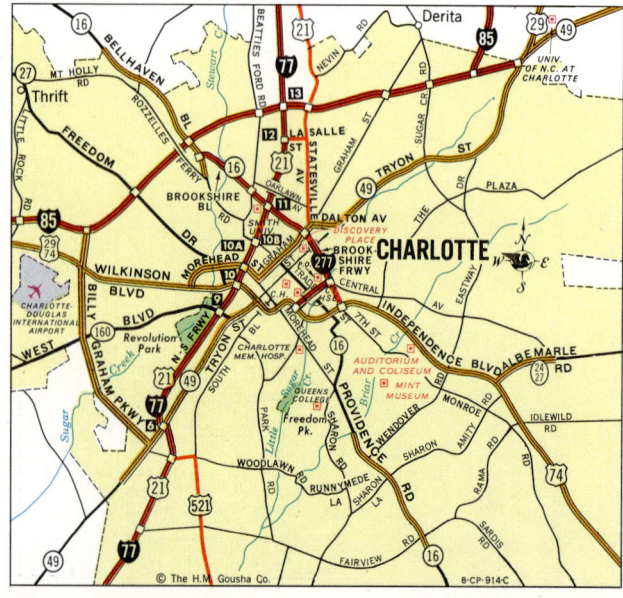

Greensboro

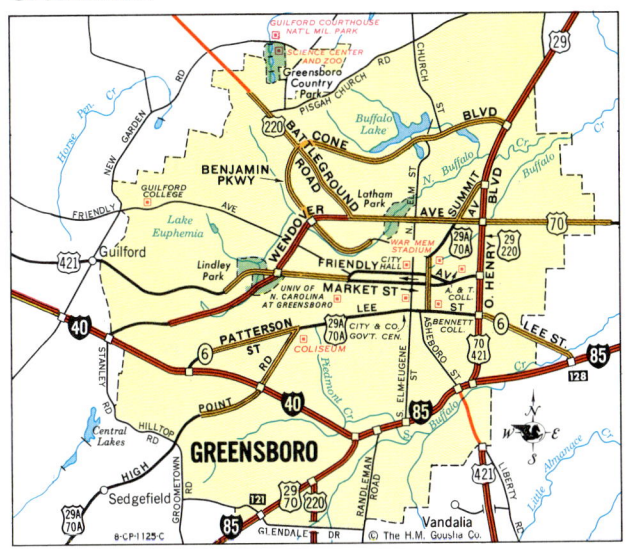

Winston-Salem

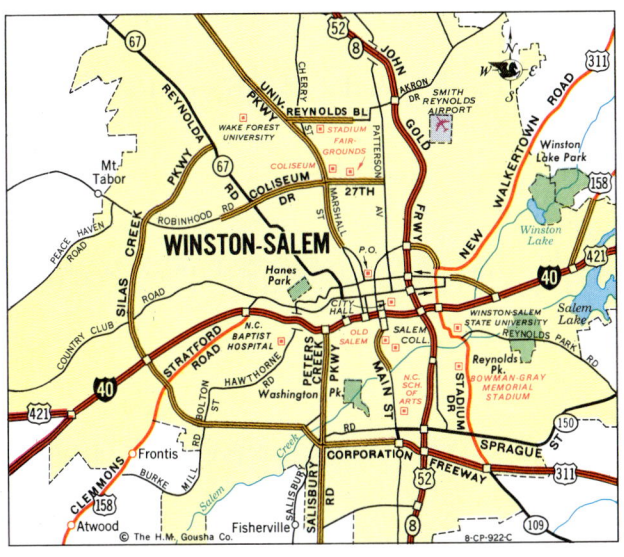

North Dakota

Grand Forks

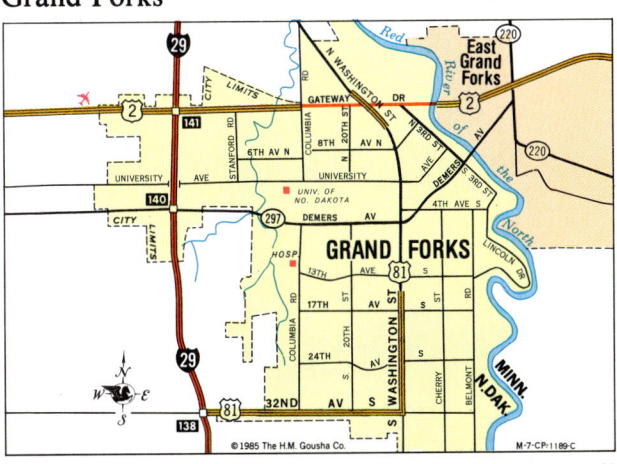

Ohio

Akron

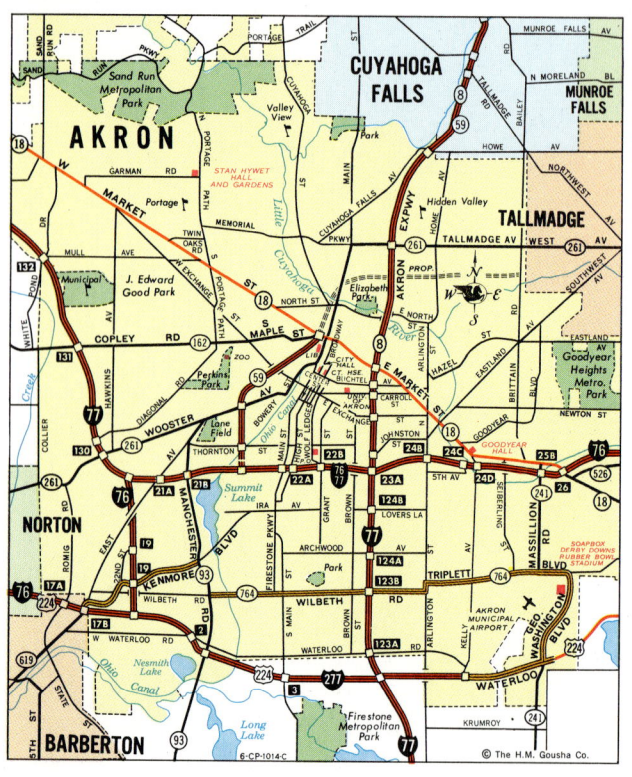

Cleveland

Cincinnati

Ohio
(continued)

Toledo

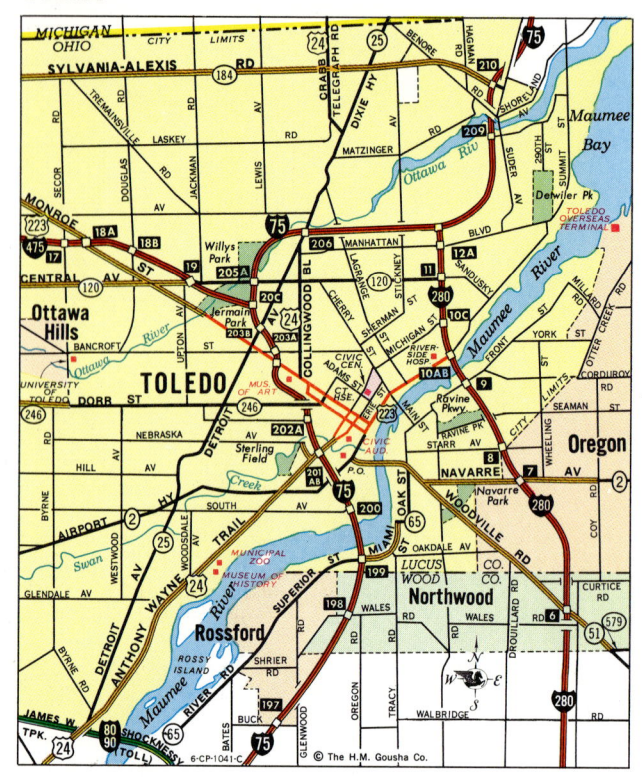

Oklahoma

Lawton

Oklahoma City

Tulsa

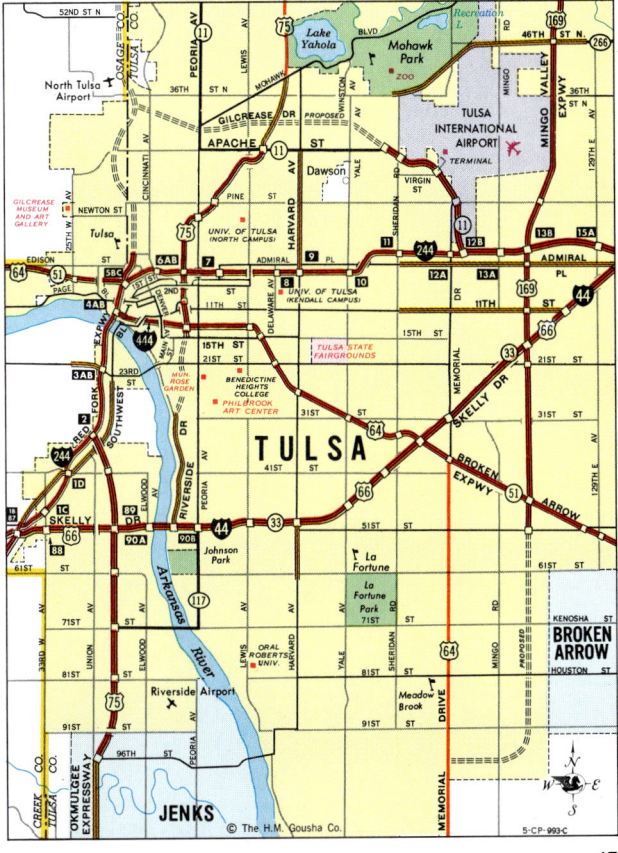

Oregon

Portland

Salem

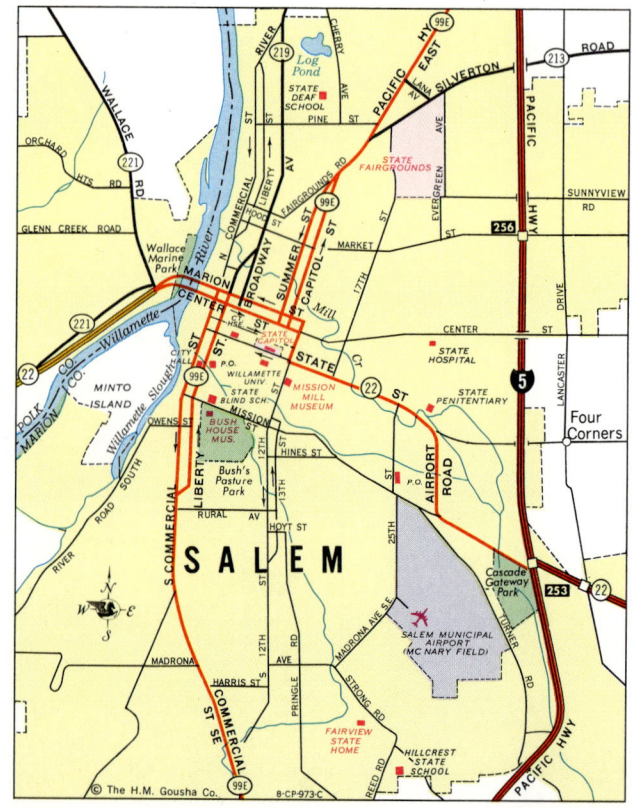

Pennsylvania

Erie

Harrisburg

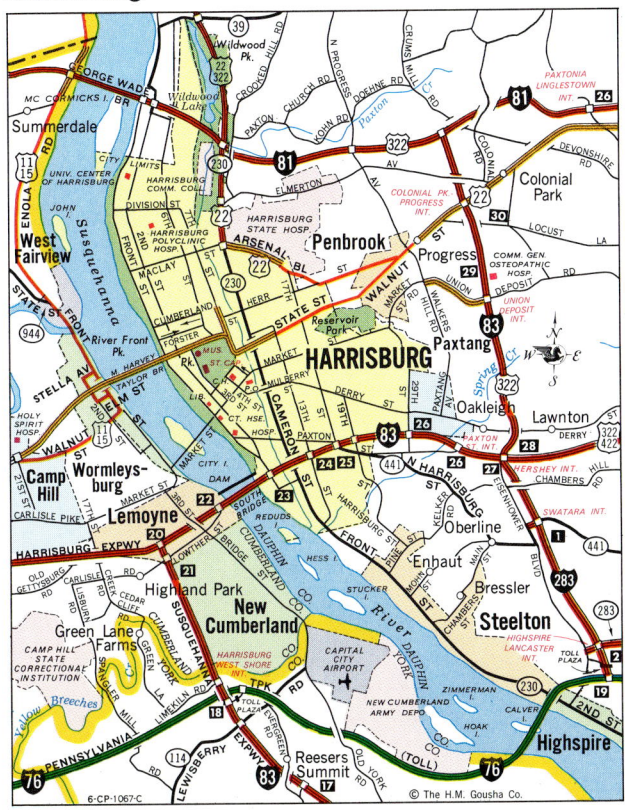

Pennsylvania
(continued)

Philadelphia

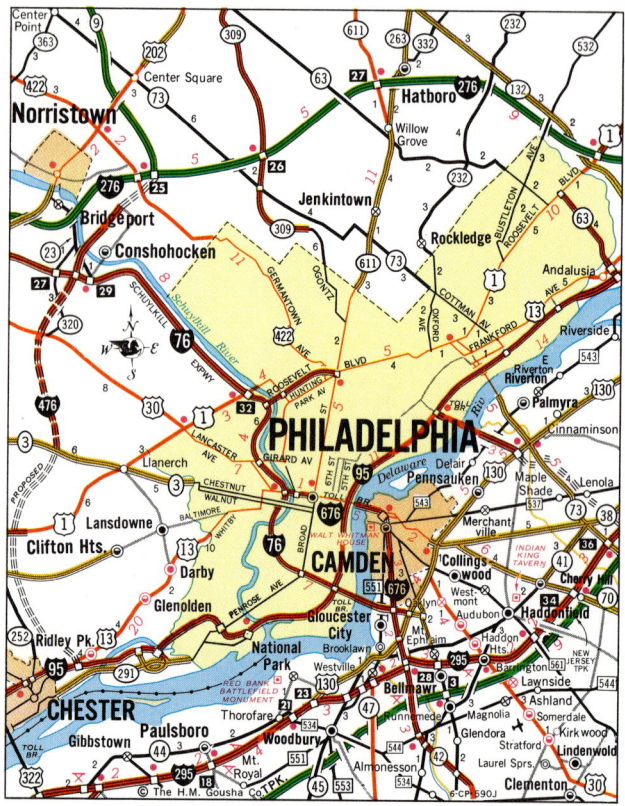

Pittsburgh

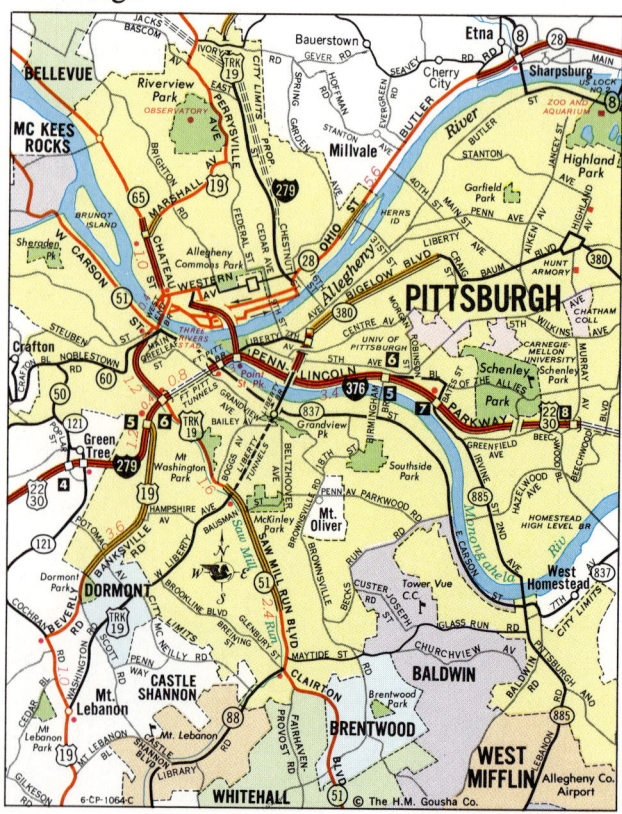

Scranton

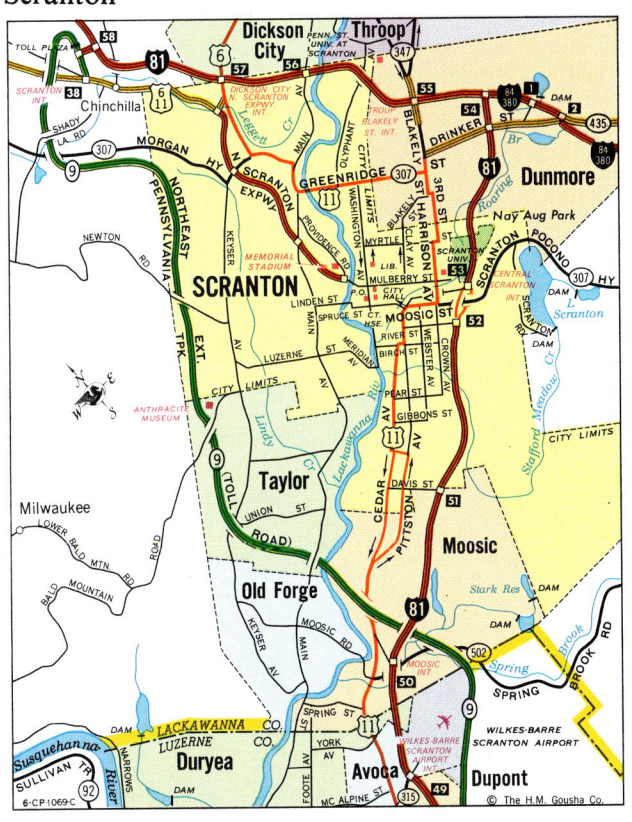

Rhode Island

Providence

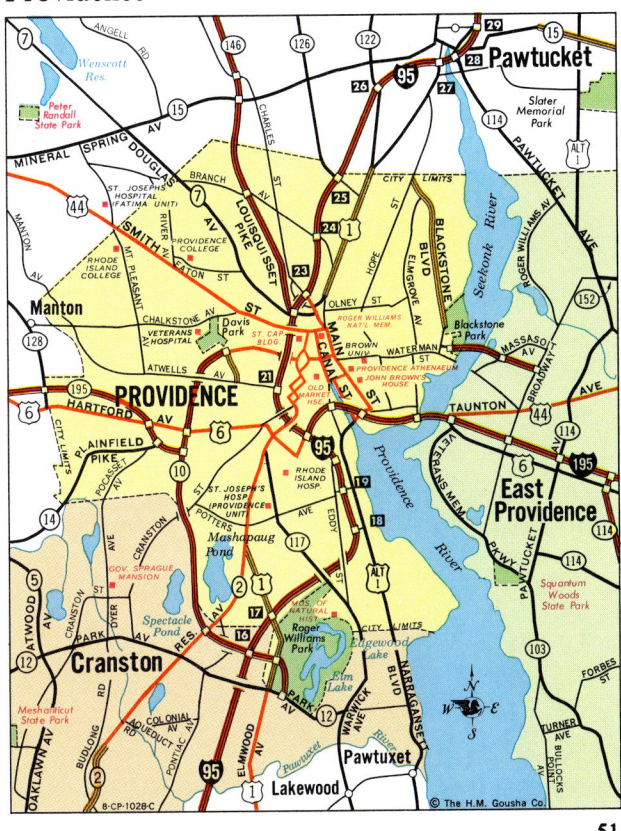

South Carolina

Charleston

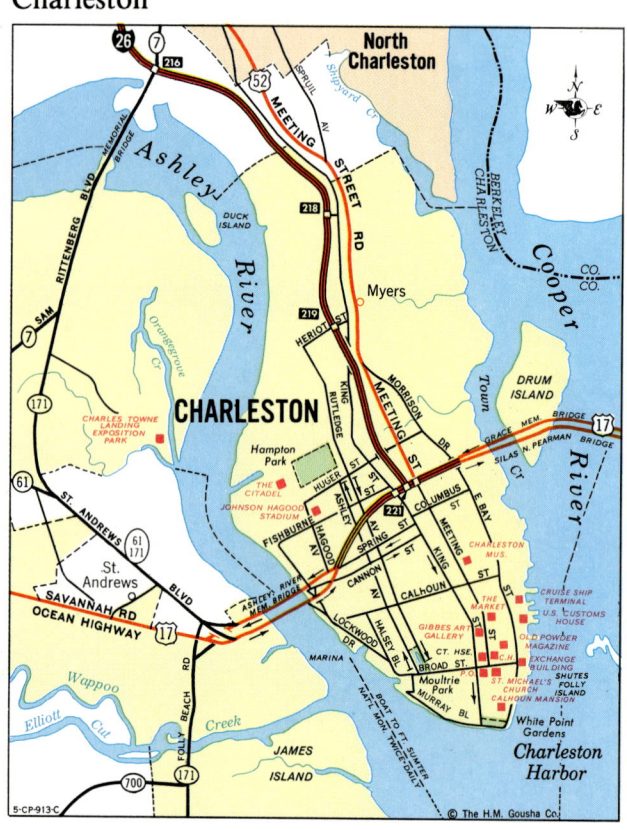

Columbia

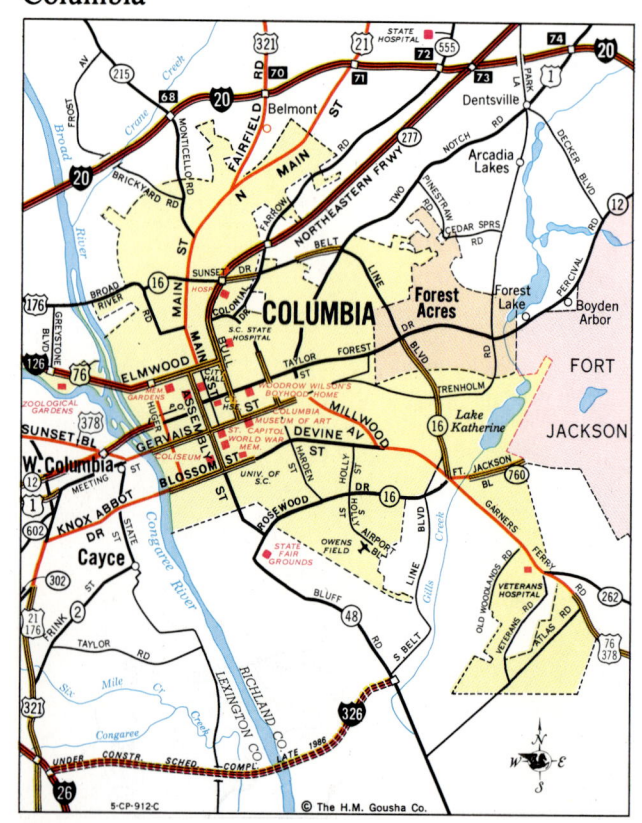

South Dakota

Rapid City

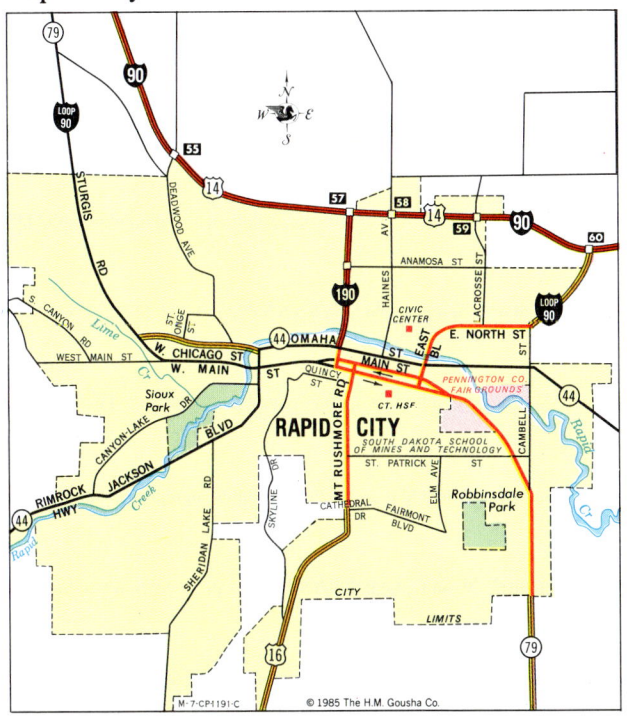

Tennessee

Chattanooga

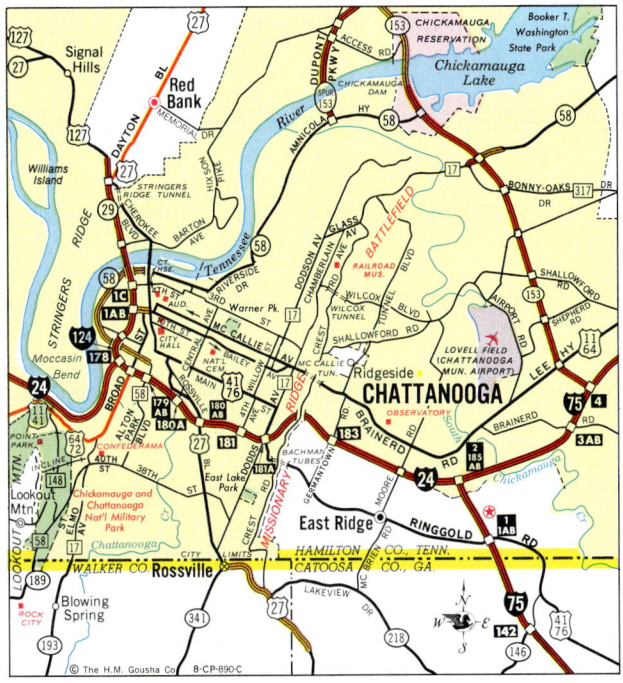

Tennessee
(continued)

Knoxville

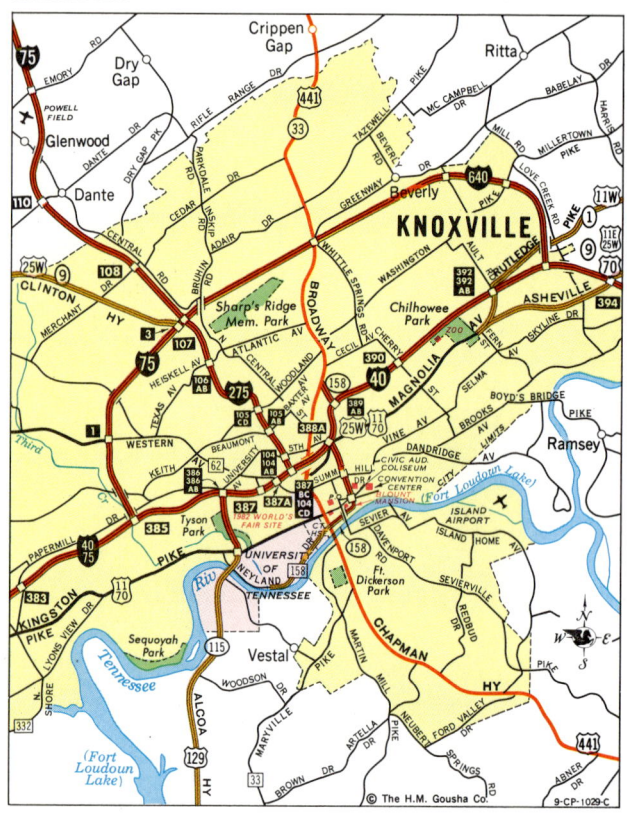

Memphis

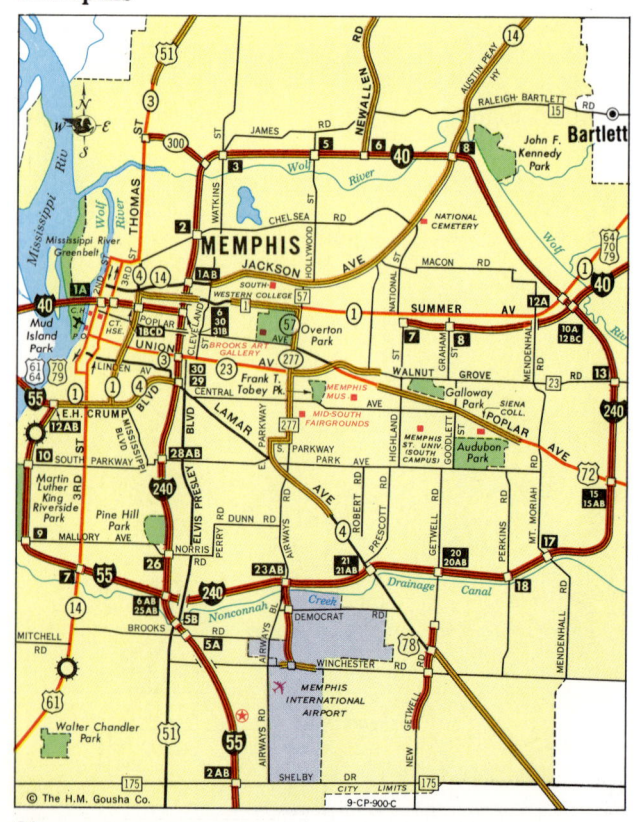

Nashville

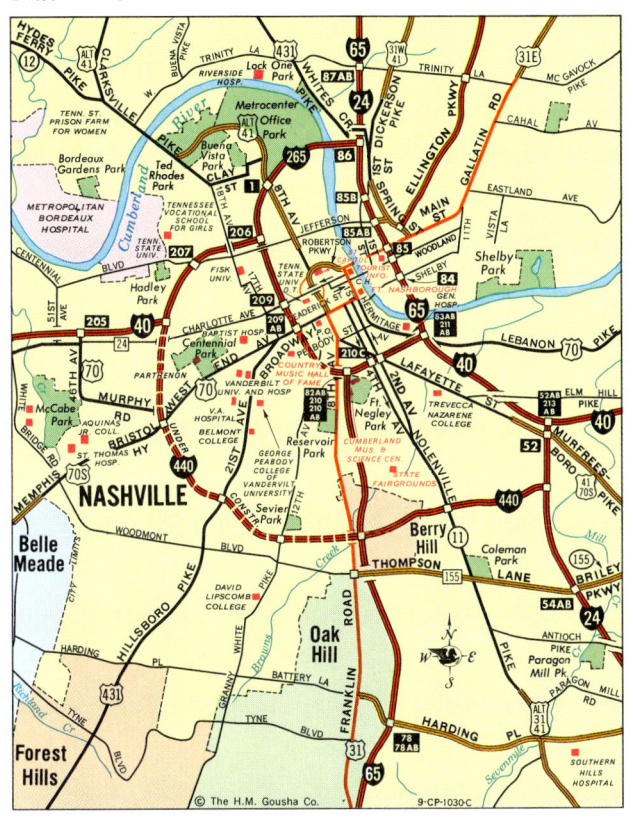

Texas

Amarillo

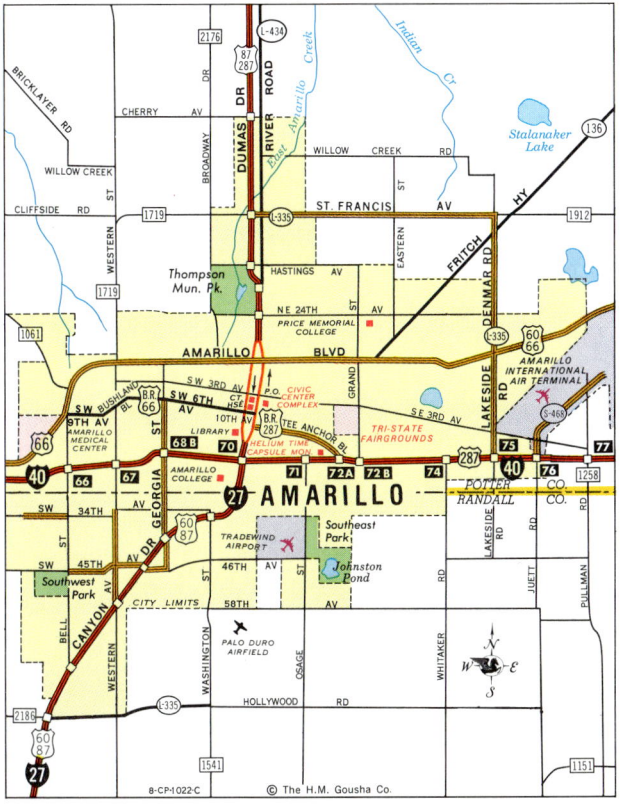

Texas
(continued)

Austin

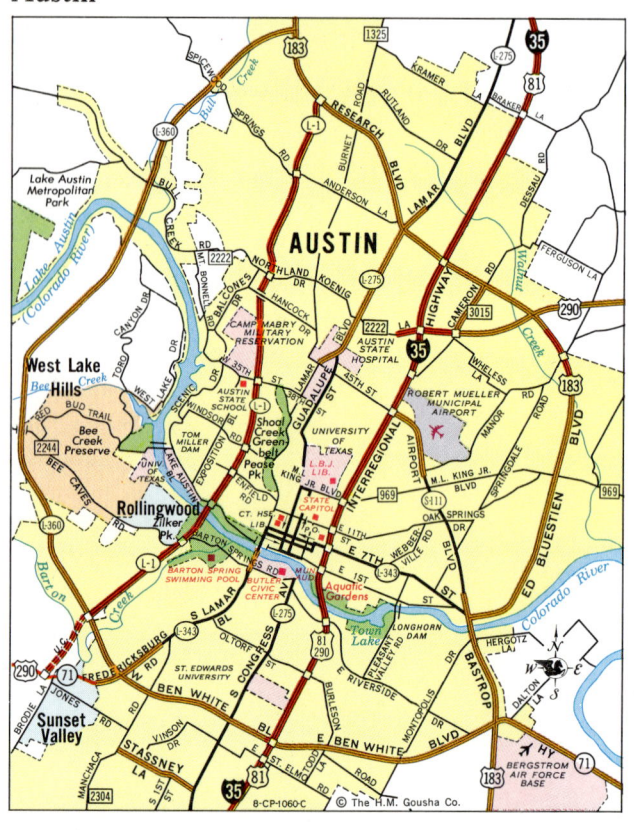

Fort Worth, Dallas

Houston

Texas
(continued)

San Antonio

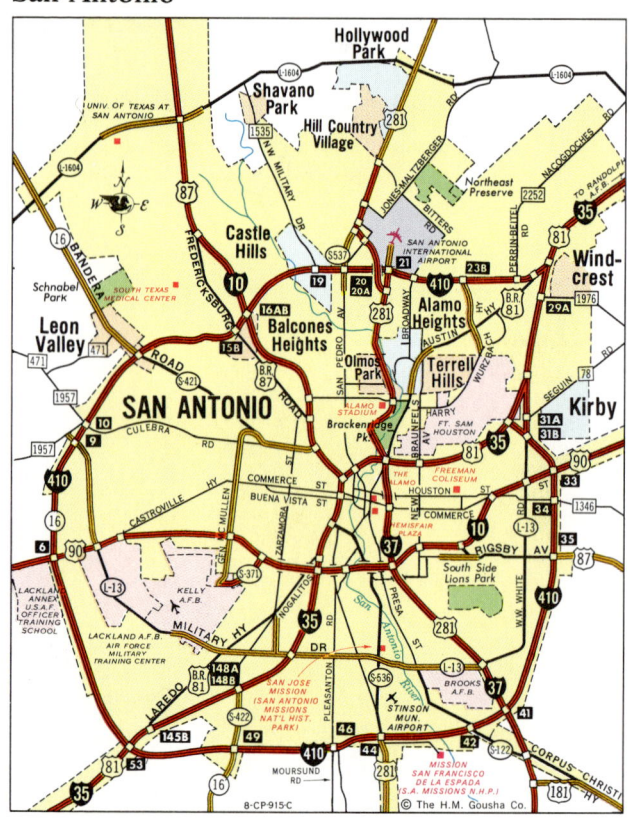

Wichita Falls

Utah

Salt Lake City

Vermont

Burlington

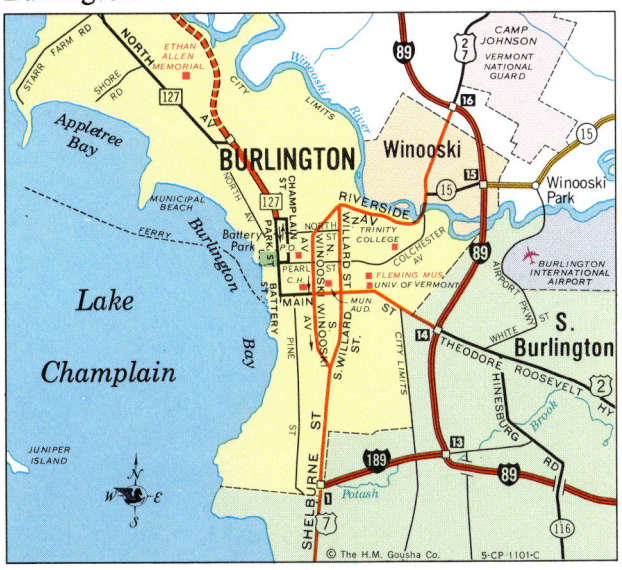

Virginia

Norfolk

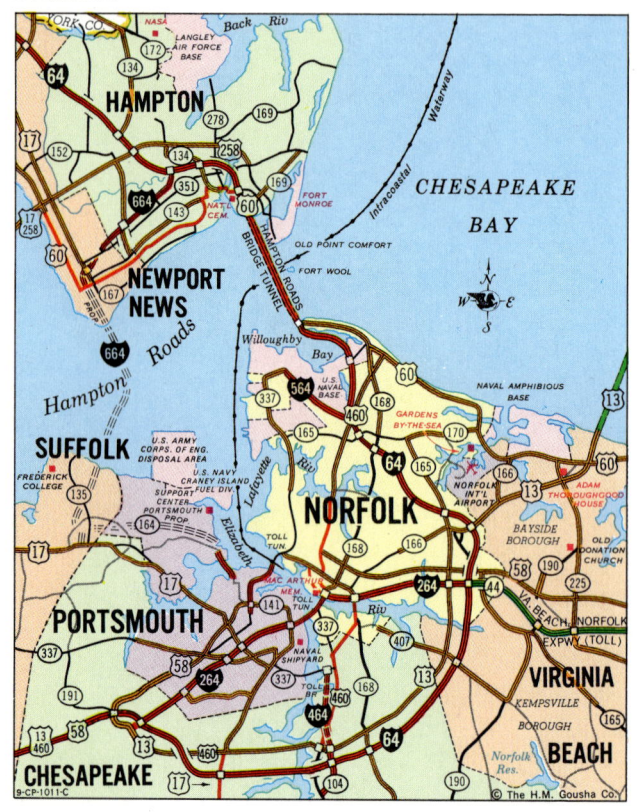

Washington

Olympia

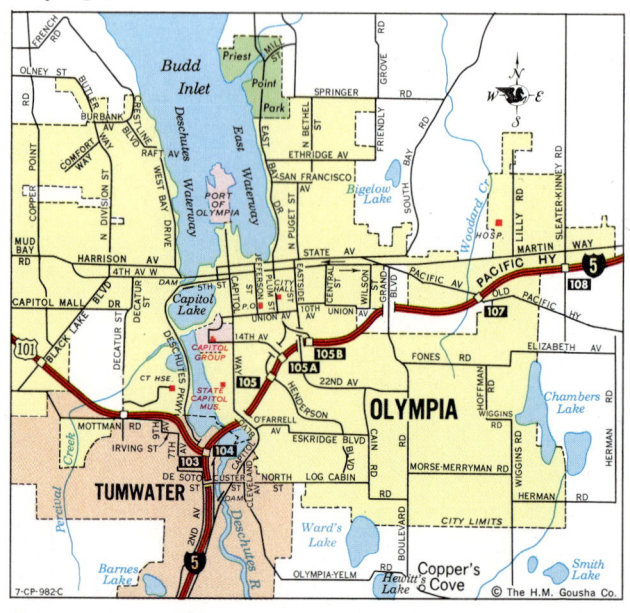

Seattle, Tacoma

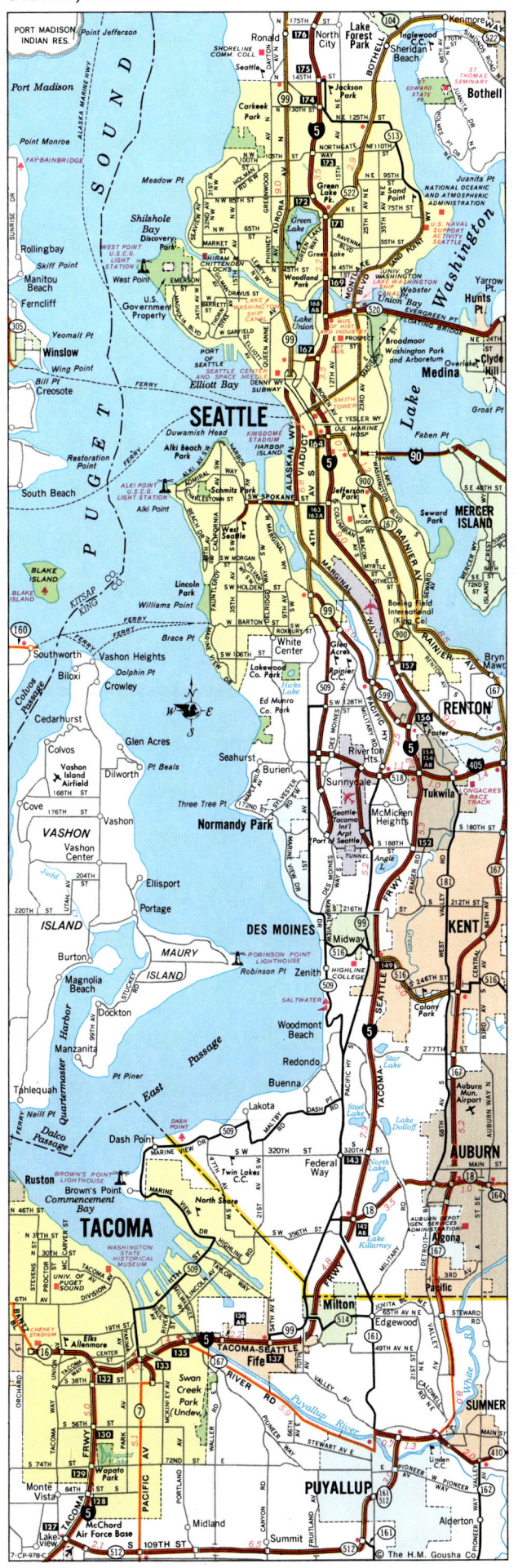

Washington
(continued)

Spokane

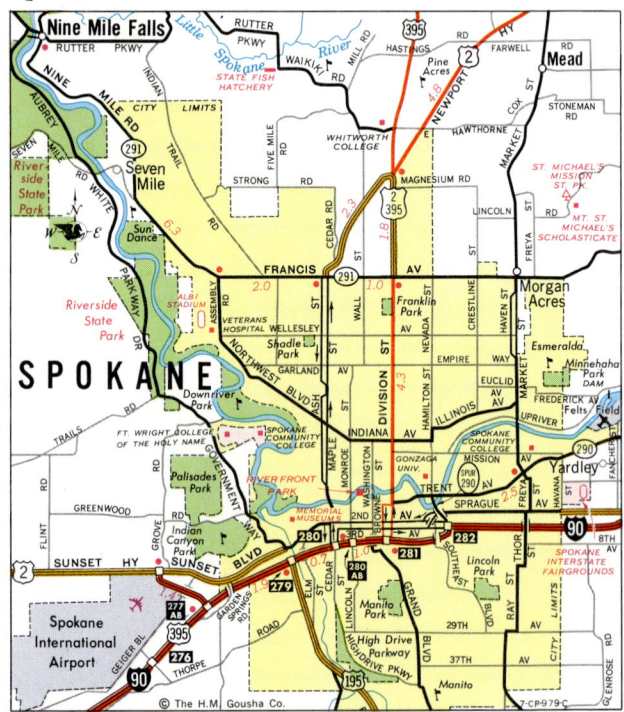

West Virginia

Charleston

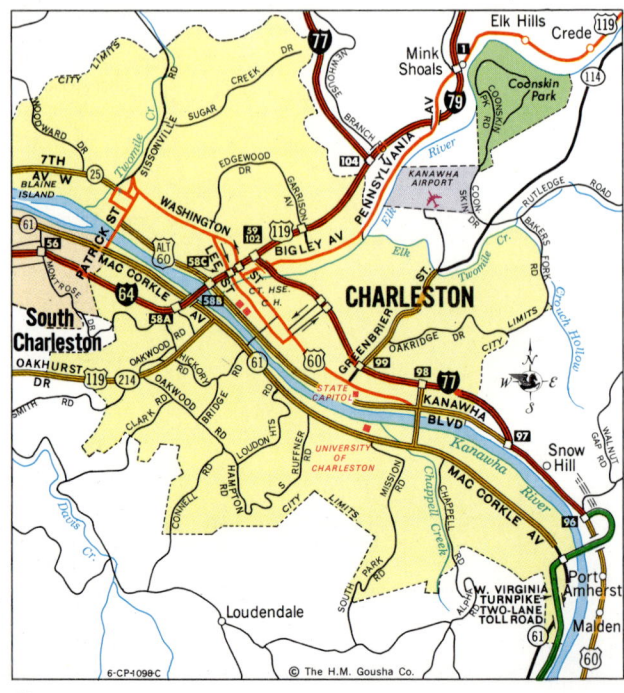

Wisconsin

Madison

Milwaukee

Wyoming

Cheyenne

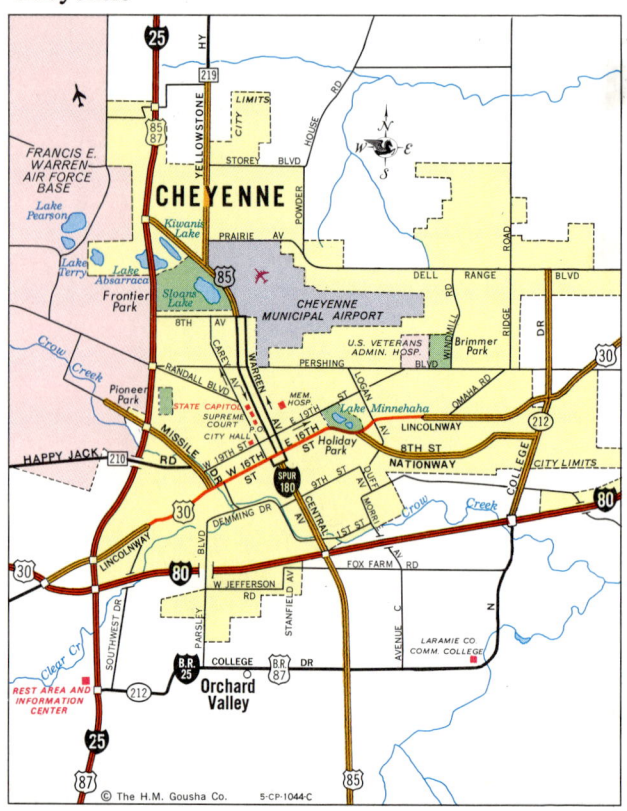

Laramie